LEARN TO DRAW UNUSUAL DINOSAURS

Welcome to Learn to Draw Unusual Dinosaurs!!!

In this book you will learn to draw all kinds unusual dinosaurs and prehistoric scenes using the 'grid method' of drawing. This method is the easiest way to learn, and when you have completed the drawings you can color all of the drawings in!

Each picture is laid out on a squared grid, and the facing page has an identical grid for you to copy the picture in, square by square. Start at the top left and work your way through the picture until you complete the cartoon. Some of these drawings can be quite challenging, so take your time and don't give up! Once you have mastered this method, you can then try drawing these cartoons on a sheet of blank paper and see how you get on!

Here are some tips to help:

•   Start using a light a pencil, so any mistakes can be erased, then go over your lines with a darker pencil or pen.

•   Focus on one box at a time, it may help to cover other boxes up with a sheet of paper so your eye is less distracted from the box you are drawing.

•   When you are finished, you can color them in to bring them to life!

Most of all, have fun!

  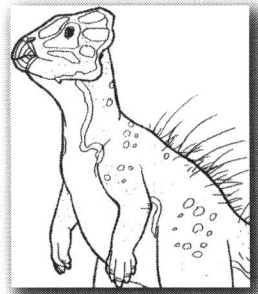 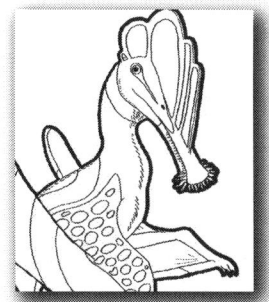

LUNASPIS

409-402.5 MYA, Early Devonian, Australia, China, Germany

This placoderm lived in shallow marine environments, and was given the name of "moon-shield" for the crescent shaped plates on either side of the head. These hunters were active swimmers, and had long, whiplike tails.

	A	B	C	D	E	F	G	H
1								
2								
3								
4								
5								
6								
7								
8								
9								
10								

DIMETRODON
295-272 MYA, Early Permian, United States and Germany

Despite being lumped in the same category as dinosaurs in countless media, Dimetrodon were not only around 40 million years before any dinosaur, but were also more closely related to mammals. The group it's in, Synapsida, also contains mammals as we know them today, and is separate from Sauropsida, which include dinosaurs. The sail-back was likely used in courtship, but probably had other uses as well.

PRIONOSUCHUS

270 MYA, Middle Permian, Brazil

This gharial-like, piscivorous amphibian lived in a humid, tropical environment. Most of them have been found to be between 2 and 2.5 meters long, but there was one individual specimen that had such a huge skull, the body would have been 9 meters long. If indeed this large, it would been one of the largest predators of the Permian.

	A	B	C	D	E	F	G	H
1								
2								
3								
4								
5								
6								
7								
8								
9								
10								

MOSCHOPS

265-260 MYA, Middle Permian, South Africa

This massive, slow-moving synapsid could grow up to 5 meters long, and fed mainly upon tough, nutrient-poor vegetation. As a result, it had to have spent most of its day eating. Its name also means "calf-face." It might have used its 10 centimeter-thick skull in dominace displays, where two individuals would push at one another with their heads.

MELANOROSAURUS

216-201 MYA, Late Triassic, South Africa

This animal was a basal sauropod, which, at about 8 meters long, was still small compared to the behemoths the future would usher in. Despite this, it had a heavily-built body, robust limbs, and a small head, which would all be traits shared by many sauropods to come.

	A	B	C	D	E	F	G	H
1								
2								
3								
4								
5								
6								
7								
8								
9								
10								

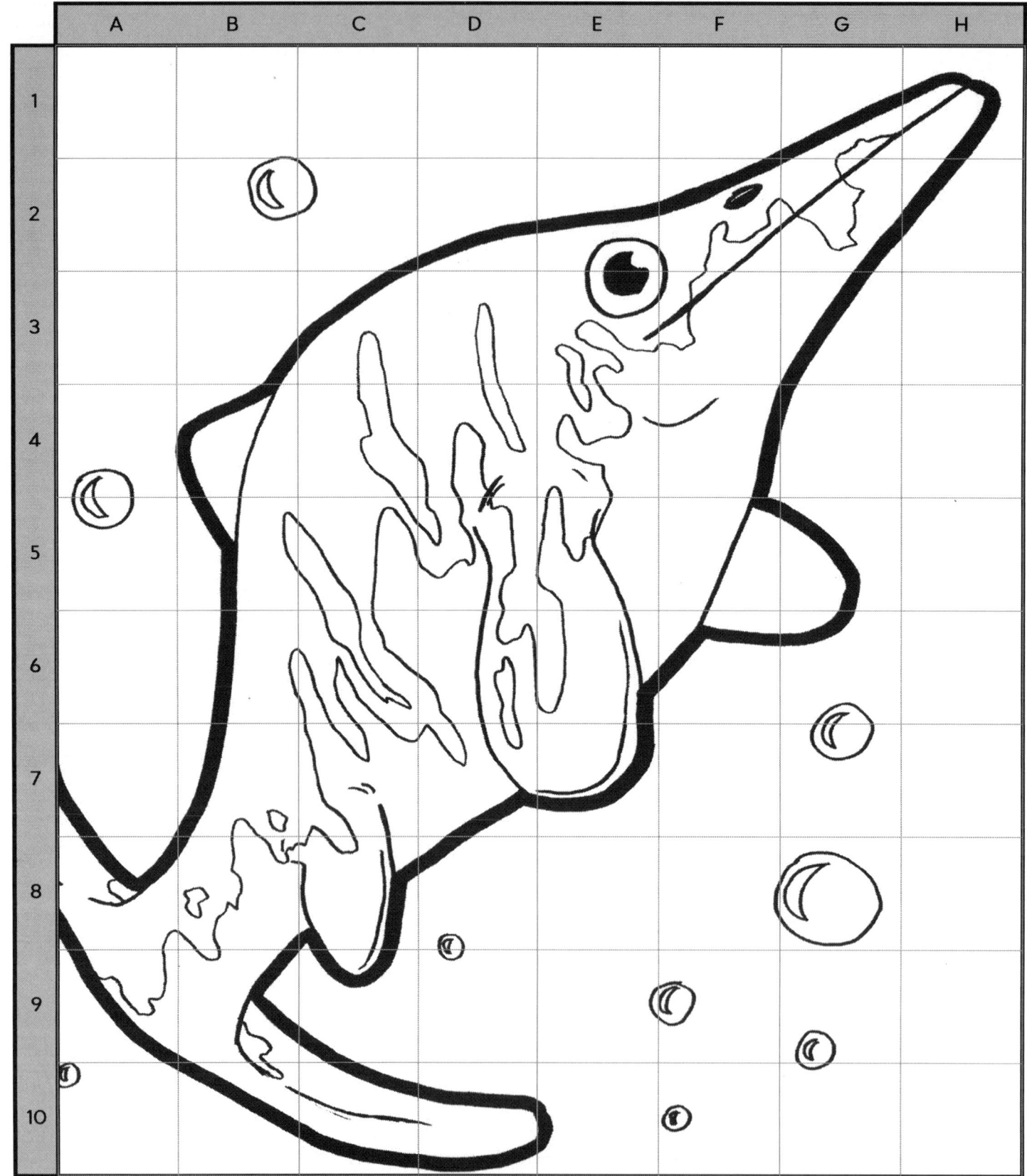

OPTHALMOSAURUS

201.5-145.5 MYA, Jurassic, England, France, Greenland, Mexico, United States

At 6 meters long, this common, dolphin-shaped squid-eater lived through almost the entire Jurassic period. Its eyes had a diameter of 23 centimeters, and took up nearly all of the space inside the skull, with even the name of this "eye-lizard" referencing their size. These huge eyes allowed them to hunt in deep waters or at night, when squid tend to be active.

	A	B	C	D	E	F	G	H
1								
2								
3								
4								
5								
6								
7								
8								
9								
10								

EORAPTOR

231 MYA, Late Triassic, Argentina

One of the first dinosaurs, eoraptor was a small, swift omnivore that stood on two legs. Its name means "dawn plunderer." During its time, dinosaurs were not yet the dominant land vertebrates they would eventually become.

LONGISQUAMA

235 MYA, Mid Triassic, Kyrgyzstan

Since its discovery, the strange structure on this animal's back has been reconstructed as a sail, a pair of gliding wings, and even as a plant that happened to be preserved on top of it. A very prominent part of this little reptile, even its name means "long scales."

	A	B	C	D	E	F	G	H
1								
2								
3								
4								
5								
6								
7								
8								
9								
10								

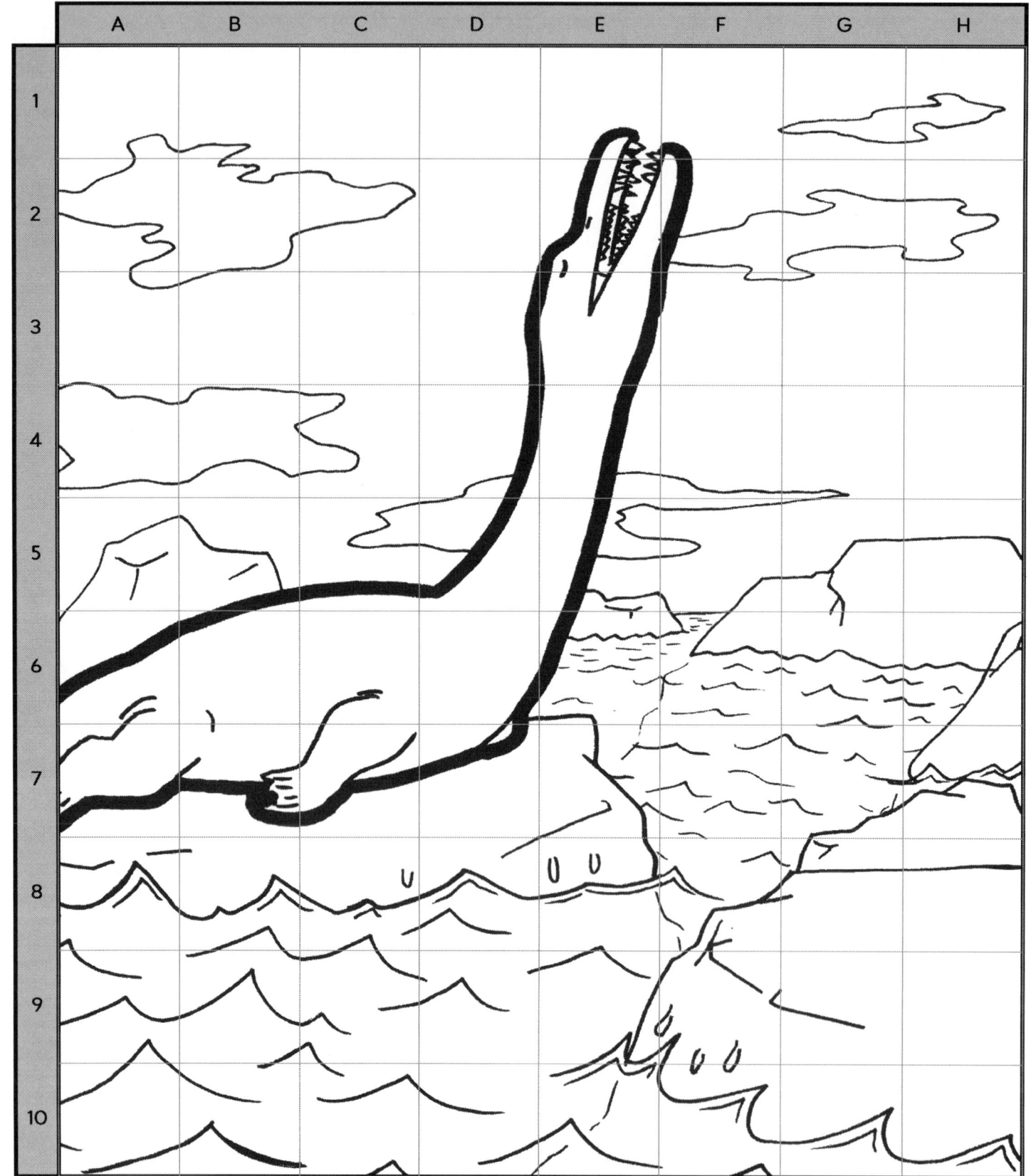

NOTHOSAURUS

240 - 210 MYA, Early to Late Triassic, Germany, Spain, China, Netherlands

Like modern-day seals, nothosaurus spent part of its time on land, and the other part in the sea. It is unknown if they gave birth to live young, or if they laid eggs, but there is evidence that suggests a common ancestor of both nothosaurs and ichthyosaurs was capable of live-births.

ATOPODENTATUS

240 MYA, Middle Triassic, Southwest China

This algae-eating marine reptile's odd, hammer-shaped head helped it root through the seafloor for food. It is the earliest known herbivorous marine reptile, which is made even more unique when compared to most other marine reptiles, which tended to be omnivores or carnivores.

TANYSROPHEUS

245 - 228 MYA, Middle Triassic, Italy and China

This was a fish-eater with a neck that was longer than both its body and tail combined, giving a total length of around 6 meters. The neck was very stiff, made up of 12-13 extremely long vertebrae. It was also not very heavy, with most of the animal's mass being near the back, where the powerful hind limbs shifted the center of mass towards the back. This allowed it to easily swing its head at prey.

COELOPHYSIS

203-196 MYA, Late Triassic to Early Jurassic, United States

This 3 meter-long speedy carnivore had eyesight akin to the hawks and eagles of today, with excellent color vision and poor low-light vision. They hunted small, fast moving prey, and may have ventured into shallow water to catch fish. Their environment consisted of floodplains with distinct wet and dry seasons.

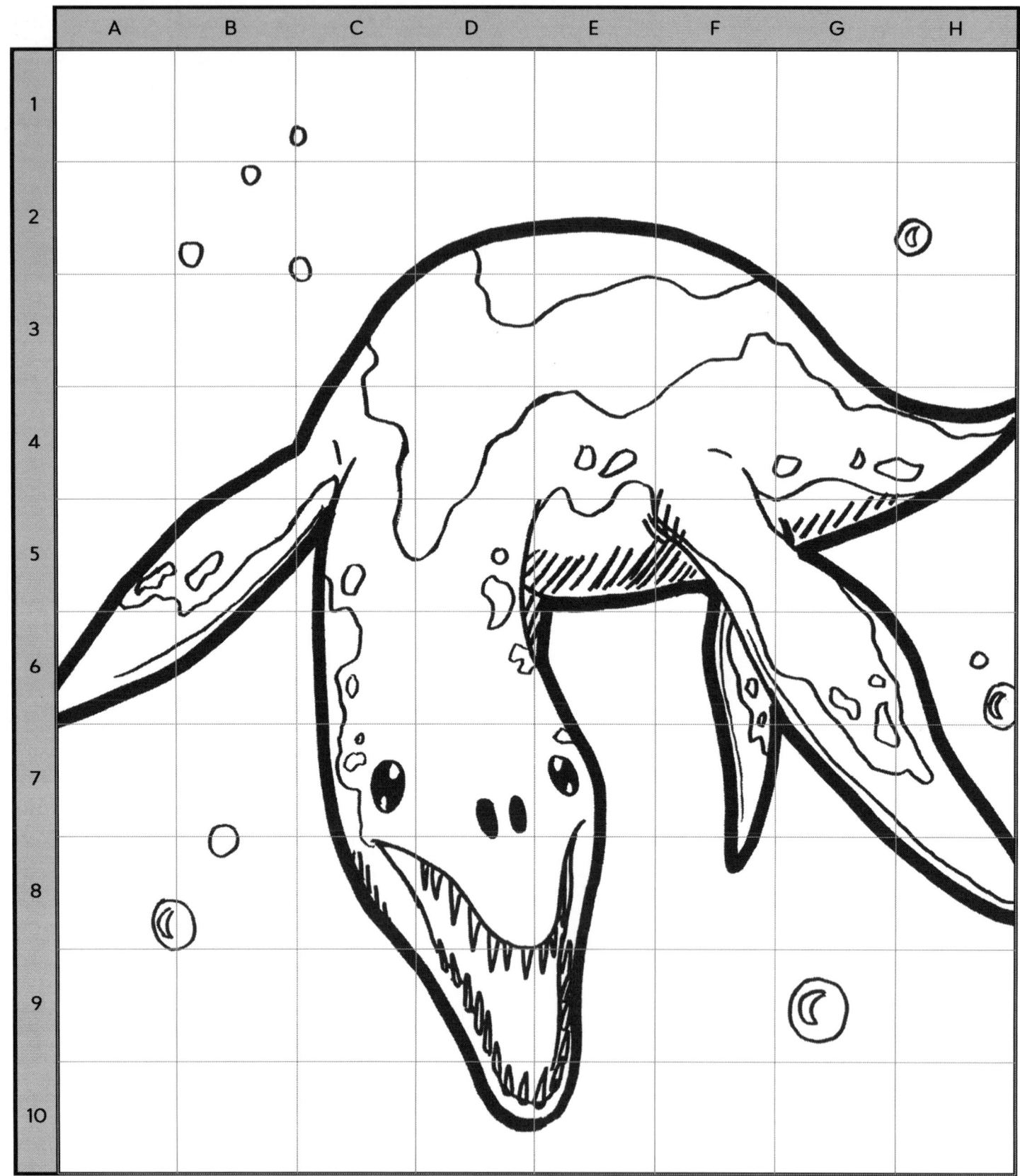

MACROPLATA

199-195 MYA, Early Jurassic, England

Compared to other pliosaurs at the time, this marine reptile had a long neck that was twice as long as its skull. It lived off a diet of fish, and used its powerful swimming muscles to lunge at individuals that broke away from synchronized shoals.

	A	B	C	D	E	F	G	H
1								
2								
3								
4								
5								
6								
7								
8								
9								
10								

BARAPASAURUS

196-183 MYA, Early Jurassic, India

A sauropod with one of the most completely known skeleton of its group in the early Jurassic, the size of Barapasaurus was comparable to later members, at around 14 meters in length. Even this early in sauropod evolution, the skeleton showed hints of developing ways of overcoming the stresses of its body's sheer weight, such as the hollowing of the vertebrae.

	A	B	C	D	E	F	G	H
1								
2								
3								
4								
5								
6								
7								
8								
9								
10								

SCUTELLOSAURUS

196 MYA, Early Jurassic, United States

This early "little shielded lizard" had several hundred osteoderms running down the length of its back and tail. Despite this, it was a small, lightly-built bipedal herbivore, at just over a meter long.

DILOPHOSAURUS

193 MYA, Early Jurassic, United States

This predator was one of the largest carnivorous dinosaurs of its time, at 7 meters in length. No significant differences have been found between fossils that would suggest dimorphism between male and female skeletal systems. Because of similarities it seems to share with spinosaurs and its proximity to water in life, it has been suggested that it was a piscivore.

	A	B	C	D	E	F	G	H
1								
2								
3								
4								
5								
6								
7								
8								
9								
10								

LIOPLEURODON

160-155 MYA, Middle to Late Jurassic, England, France, Germany, Argentina, Mexico

Many specimens of this Jurassic apex predator have been discovered. Its head was a fifth of the total size of its body, and was filled with long and strong conical teeth. It used its sense of smell to find its prey, which it would ambush in a quick burst of speed.

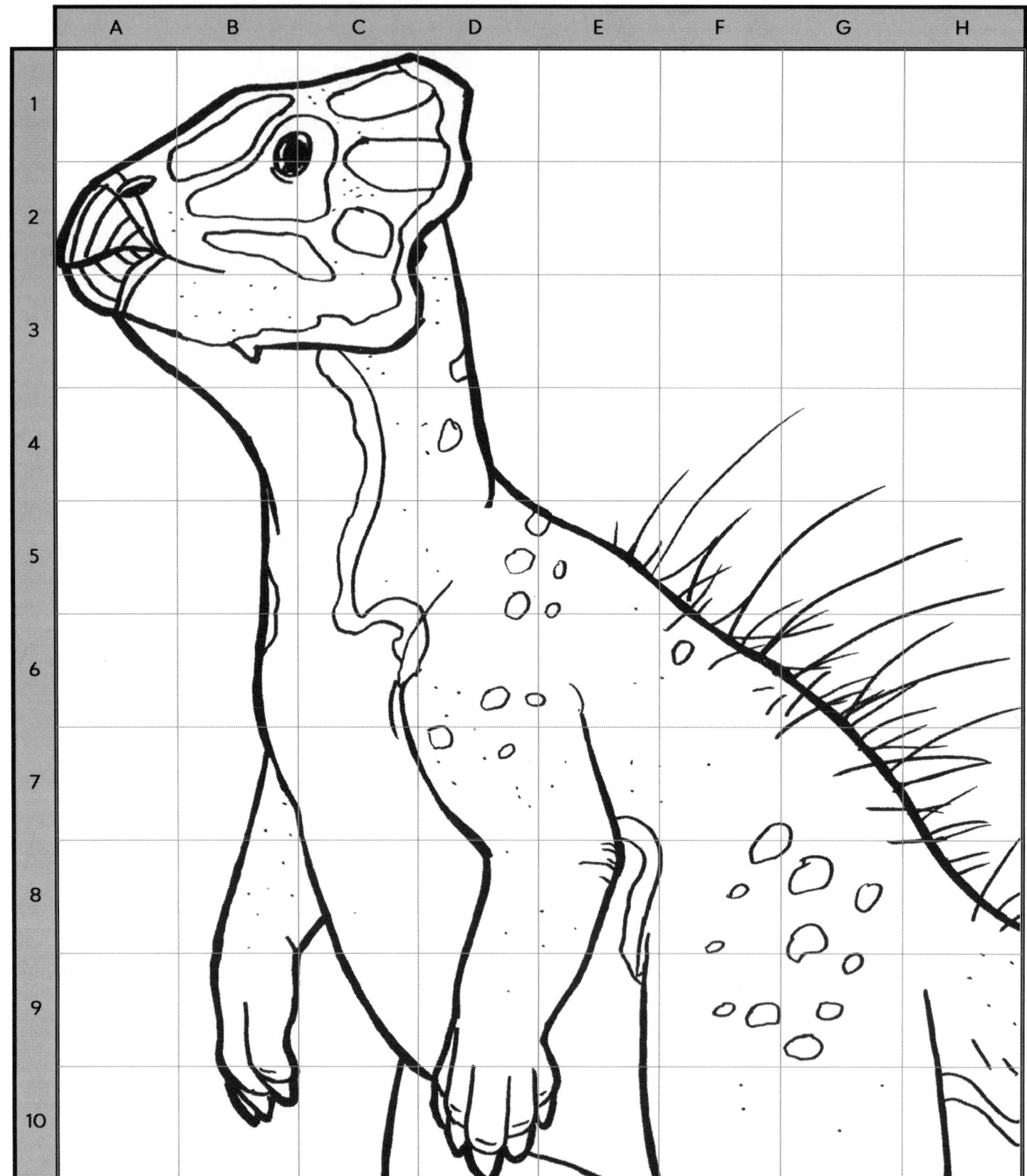

YINLONG

158 MYA, Late Jurassic, China

At just over a meter long, this ancestor to the ceratopsians was much smaller than many of its future descendants. The crest wasn't nearly as pronounced as it would become in time, and this little generalist herbivore was still a bipedal dinosaur. It might have had a set of quills along its tail and back, as some later species would be discovered with evidence of such.

ALLOSAURUS

155-150 MYA, Late Jurassic, United States, Portugal

A large bipedal predator averaging 8.5 meters in length, Allosaurus is one of the better-known, and more common, theropods. It wasn't as built for speed as other theropods, but was better suited as an ambush predator in its semiarid, floodplain, environment.

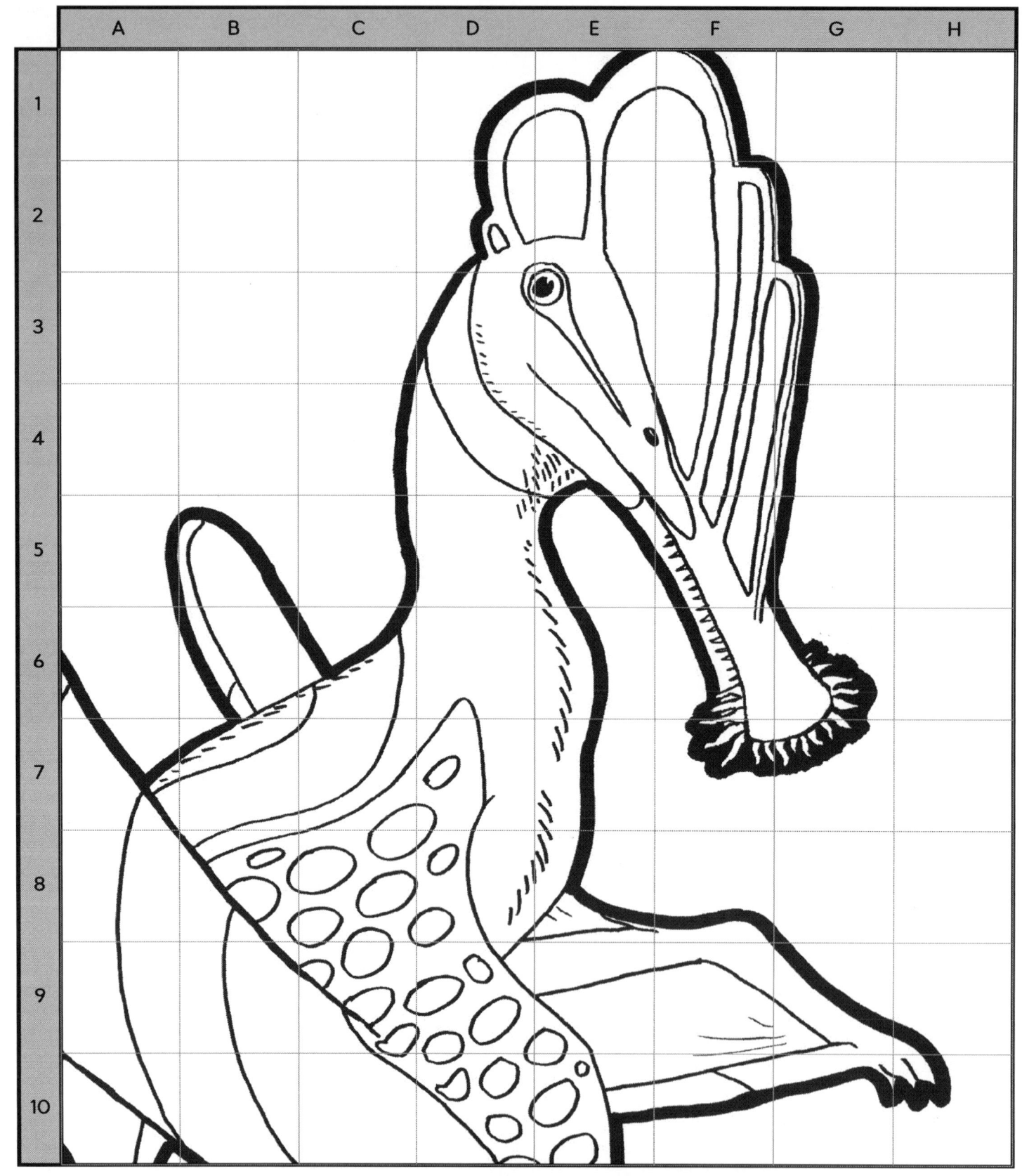

GNATHOSAURUS

152-145 MYA, Late Jurassic, England and Germany

This filter-feeder's wingspan was on the smaller end of the spectrum for a pterosaur, at 1.75 meters across. It lived right up to the end of the Jurassic, and was originally thought to have been a prehistoic crocodile when first discovered.

BARYONYX

130-125 MYA, Late Cretaceous, England, Spain, Portugal

Baryonyx were specialized in catching and eating fish, and it used both its teeth and the "heavy claw" on its hands to aquire prey. It was probably not limited to eating fish, as pterosaur and Iguandon remains have been found with evidence of predation or scavenging.

KRONOSAURUS

129-99 MYA, Early Cretaceous, Australia and Columbia

Kronosaurus was one of the largest pliosaurs, reaching a length of up to 10 meters. Its name means "lizard of Cronus," the figure being one of the titans from ancient Greek mythology. A fast and powerful swimmer, it preyed on plesiosaurs, turtles, fish, and squid.

IGUANODON

126-125 MYA, Early Cretaceous, North Africa, Belgium, England, Germany, United States

Iguanodon were herbivores that were capable of moving in either a two-legged or four-legged way. They averaged 10 meters in length. Each front foot had a spiked thumb they could have used to defend themselves with (or for getting into seeds and nuts), while the little finger was flexible and allowed the animal to grasp and manipulate objects.

	A	B	C	D	E	F	G	H
1								
2								
3								
4								
5								
6								
7								
8								
9								
10								

YUTYRANNUS

124 MYA, Early Cretaceous, China

This large tyrannosauroid is the largest member of the group to have been confirmed to have been covered in feathers. Because of the climate they lived in, this covering was likely used primarily as insulation against the cold environment. They were large, bipedal predators capable of reaching sizes of up to 9 meters long.

HUAXIAPTERUS

120 MYA, Early Cretaceous, China

This small tapejarid pterosaur shared a few traits with the earlier rhamphorhynchoids, and spent much of its time on the ground.
It has been found with much of the skeleton intact, allowing for more accurate, and more confident reconstructions.
In addition, the area it was discovered (the Jiufotang Formation) contained many other pterosaur fossils, making it a species-rich site.

	A	B	C	D	E	F	G	H
1								
2								
3								
4								
5								
6								
7								
8								
9								
10								

ELASMOSAURUS

80 MYA, Late Cretaceous, United States and Canada

At over 10 meters long, this was one of the largest plesiosaurs. Plesiosaurs generally had long necks, equally sized paddles, short tails, and gave birth to live young. Elasmosaurus had 72 neck vertebrae, and such a long neck helped it get close to the small fish and squid on which it preyed. Stones have also been found in the stomach area, indicating it had swallowed them to help with digestion.

	A	B	C	D	E	F	G	H
1								
2								
3								
4								
5								
6								
7								
8								
9								
10								

PARASAUROLOPHUS

76-74 MYA, Late Cretaceous, United States and Canada

Like other hadrosaurs, this dinosaur could be bipedal or quadrupedal. These animals were rare in the fossil record. Their dental battery was suited for grinding up tough plants, and worn down teeth were simply replaced. The crest has been given a variety of uses over the years, including display, sound production, a snorkle-like function, and scent detection, though most are outdated.

STYRACOSAURUS

75 MYA, Late Cretaceous, United States and Canada

This "spiked lizard" lived in herds, and used its beak to eat tough vegetation. Its mouth was filled with a dental battery of teeth that were constantly replaced as they got worn down by slicing vegetable matter. Because of its relative fragility, the extensive horn and frills might have been used in display rather than defense, though they might have made the animal appear larger to potential predators.

	A	B	C	D	E	F	G	H
1								
2								
3								
4								
5								
6								
7								
8								
9								
10								

SALTASAURUS

70 MYA, Late Cretaceous, Argentina

This dinosaur was the first to be discovered bearing osteoderms, bony plates of armor embedded in the skin. Earlier, sauropods were thought to have been protected from predators due to their sheer size, but it seems that further defenses were needed for the survival of the smaller ones. Though they were estimated to have been between 8.5 and 12 meters long, this is still very small for a sauropod.

PACHYCEPHALOSAURUS

70-66 MYA, Late Cretaceous, United States amd Canada

One of the last non-avian dinosaurs before the Cretaceous mass-extinction, this "thick-headed lizard" was a medium-sized herbivore.
As the animal aged, the horns and spikes would gradually reduce in size, while the dome top and rounded skull knobs grew.
The dome has been thought to have been used in display, defense, and/or same-species head-butting, but more research is needed.

	A	B	C	D	E	F	G	H
1								
2								
3								
4								
5								
6								
7								
8								
9								
10								

HATZEGOPTERYX

66 MYA, Late Cretaceous, Romania

This giant azdharchid pterosaur lived right up to the end of the Cretaceous. The skull alone was 3 meters long, and the wingspan stretched 12 meters wide. It was a terrestrial foraging predator, though this by far did not mean it was flightless. It played the role of apex predator of Hateg Island, preying upon larger dinosaurs than what other pterosaurs could handle.

SEBECUS

56-50 MYA, Eocene, Argentina, Bolivia

Sebecus had an oddly-shaped skull among crocodyliforms. Instead of the skull being raised up where the eyes are, the top of the head was level. Also unlike the familiar alligators and crocodiles of today, it was entirely terrestrial. It had longer legs than its water-dwelling cousins, and eyes on the sides of the head instead of on top.

GASTORNIS

56-45 MYA, Paleogene, China, North America, Western Europe

This dinosaur was a large, flightless bird. Originally assumed to have used its impressive beak to disembowel small prey, new speculation points to the powerful jaws being used to crack open nuts and seeds, rather than animal bones. Predatory dinosaurs tend to also have curved, pointed claws, which these birds lacked, and the lack of a hooked beak further suggested herbivory.

	A	B	C	D	E	F	G	H
1								
2								
3								
4								
5								
6								
7								
8								
9								
10								

EDAPHOSAURUS

300 - 280 MYA, Late Carboniferous to Early Permian, Germany, Czech Republic, and United States

These animals were some of the earliest large, plant-eating amniote tetrapods. Like many other sail-backed animals, many different uses were proposed for the sail, including but not limited to: courtship, thermoregulation, fat storage, muscle support, camouflage, protection against predators, and species recognition. It's likely the sail had more than one purpose.

	A	B	C	D	E	F	G	H
1								
2								
3								
4								
5								
6								
7								
8								
9								
10								

LYCAENOPS

270-251 MYA, Mid to Late Permian, South Africa

This "wolf-face" was a carnivorous therapsid, and were about a meter long, and weighed about 15 kilograms. Being in the same group as mammals, they were likely covered in fur, and could hold their legs under their body rather than splayed to the sides. This allowed them to outrun other animals.

HIMALAYASAURUS

215.5-212 MYA, Late Triassic, Tibet

This giant ichthyosaur could reach a length of up to 15 meters, though it is only known from fragmentary remains. It was in the family Shastasauridae, which also included Shonisaurus. Unlike other ichthyosaurs, which had pointed, conical teeth, Himalayasaurus's teeth were large, flat, and suitable for cutting.

EUDIMORPHODON

210 - 203 MYA, Late Triassic, Italy, France, Luxembourg

A small pterosaur with a wingspan of just over a meter, its teeth had the best fit of all other pterosaurs when its mouth was closed. It is one of the most abundant fossils in Italy. It was also one of the earliest pterosaurs, and like many early members of the group, was a piscivore.

	A	B	C	D	E	F	G	H
1								
2								
3								
4								
5								
6								
7								
8								
9								
10								

KULINDADROMEUS

169-144 MYA, Middle to Late Jurassic, Russia

This little herbivore was 1.5 meters long, and had a body covered by a layer of dinofuzz, while its tail had a scaley covering. This discovery of an ornithischian dinosaur having a feathery coat points at this trait originating in a shared common ancestor of both bird-hipped and lizard-hipped groups of dinosaur, rather than being exclusive to the theropods.

	A	B	C	D	E	F	G	H
1								
2								
3								
4								
5								
6								
7								
8								
9								
10								

YI

160 MYA, Middle Jurassic, China

Yi is not only notable for having the shortest genus name of any dinosaur, but for the way its wings are presented. Yi had a feathery coating, and bones at its wrist supported a membrane that may have been used in gliding, with some flapping to control its descent. This was a very small dinosaur, weighing less than 400 grams.

	A	B	C	D	E	F	G	H
1								
2								
3								
4								
5								
6								
7								
8								
9								
10								

KENTROSAURUS

155-150 MYA, Late Jurassic, Tanzania

This 4.5 meter long stegosaur had a front half that was adorned with two rows of standing plates, and a back half that sported two rows of spikes. Being a smaller member of the group, and having a center of mass that was unusually far back for a quadruped, it was able to rear up on its hind limbs to reach food that was higher up. This trait also allowed it to quickly pivot, swinging the spiked tail at its attacker.

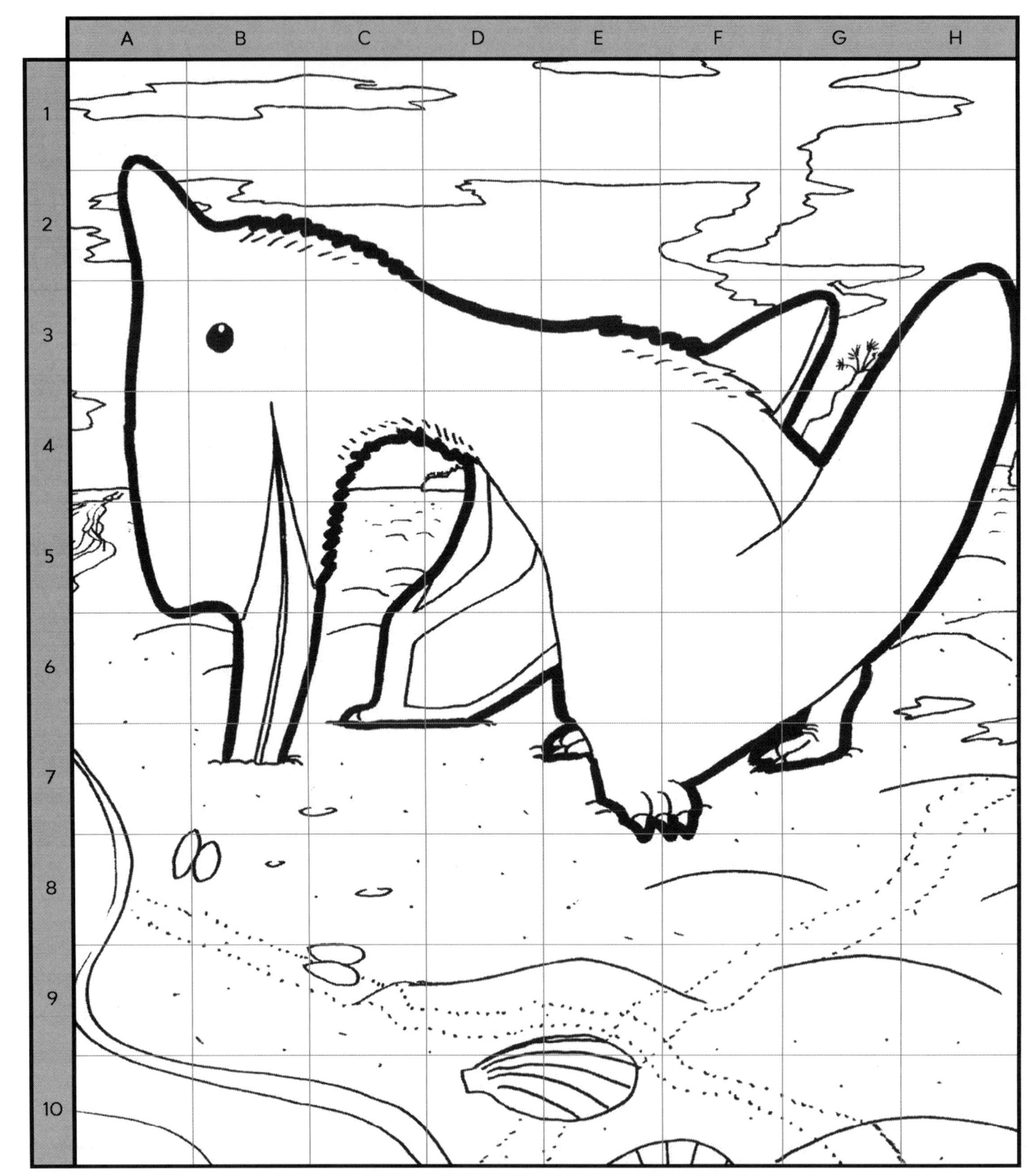

DSUNGARIPTERUS

130 MYA, Early Cretaceous, China and Mongolia

The upcurved, pointed jaws and flat back teeth of this pterosaur were ideal for feeding on mussels, snails, and even small vertebrates.
It would extract the invertebrate from the mud or sand with the curve of its beak, and then crush it with the back teeth.
It was a medium-sized animal, with a wingspan of around 3.5 meters.

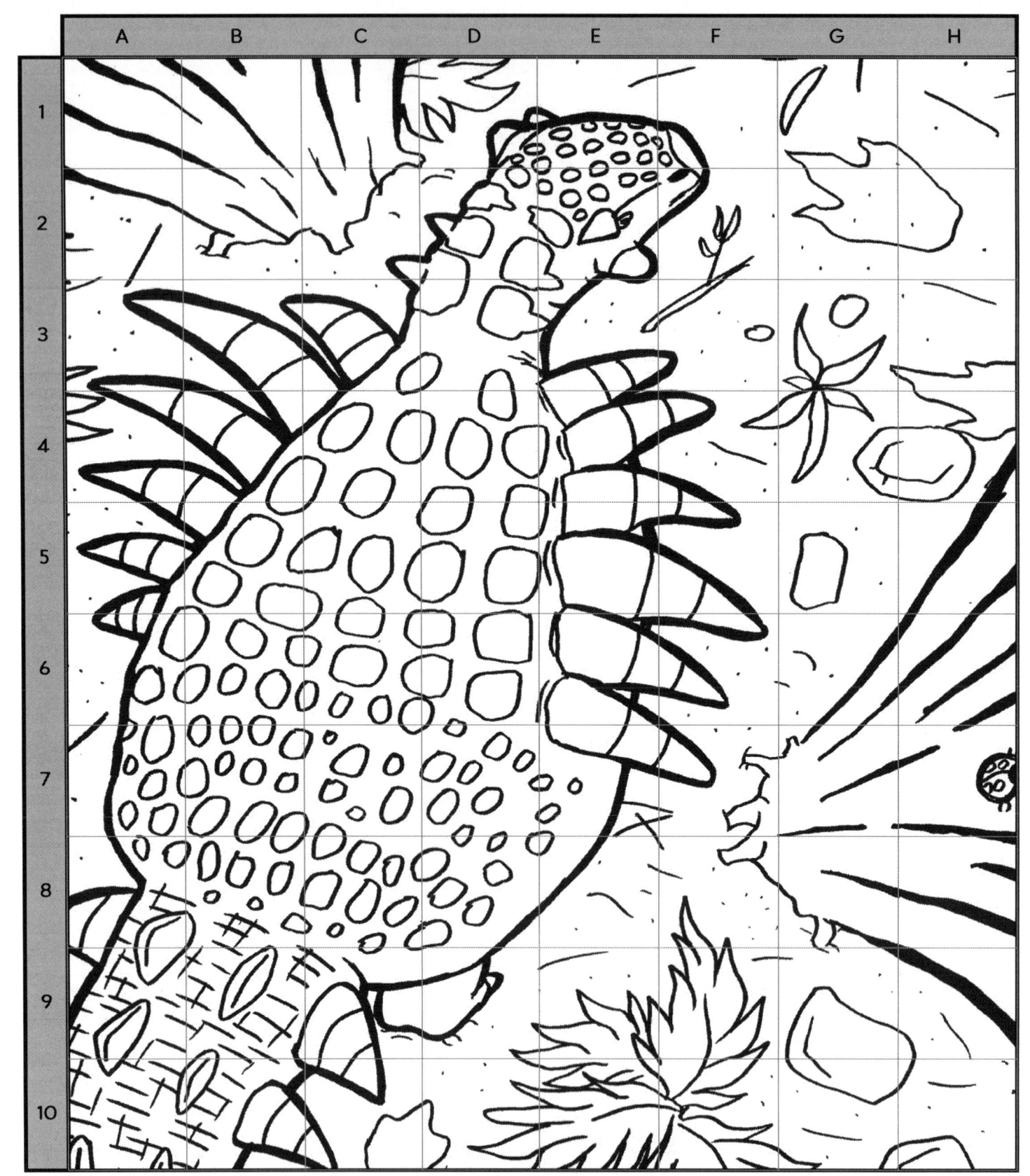

GASTONIA

126 MYA, Early Cretaceous, North America

This 5 meter-long herbivore was heavily-armored was abundant in the partly wooded areas it inhabited.
Unlike some ankylosaurs, Gastonia lacked a tail club, and instead defended itself with rows of bony spikes protruding out from the back.
Even for this group of dinosaurs, its limbs were short, and it was wide around the middle.

	A	B	C	D	E	F	G	H
1								
2								
3								
4								
5								
6								
7								
8								
9								
10								

TAPEJARA

112 MYA, Mid Cretaceous, Brazil

A smaller pterosaur with a wingspan of around 3.5 meters, its head supported a long bony crest, which itself supported an even larger crest made of softer tissue. It likely lived off of fruits, insects, and maybe vertebrates, living as an omnivore or herbivore.

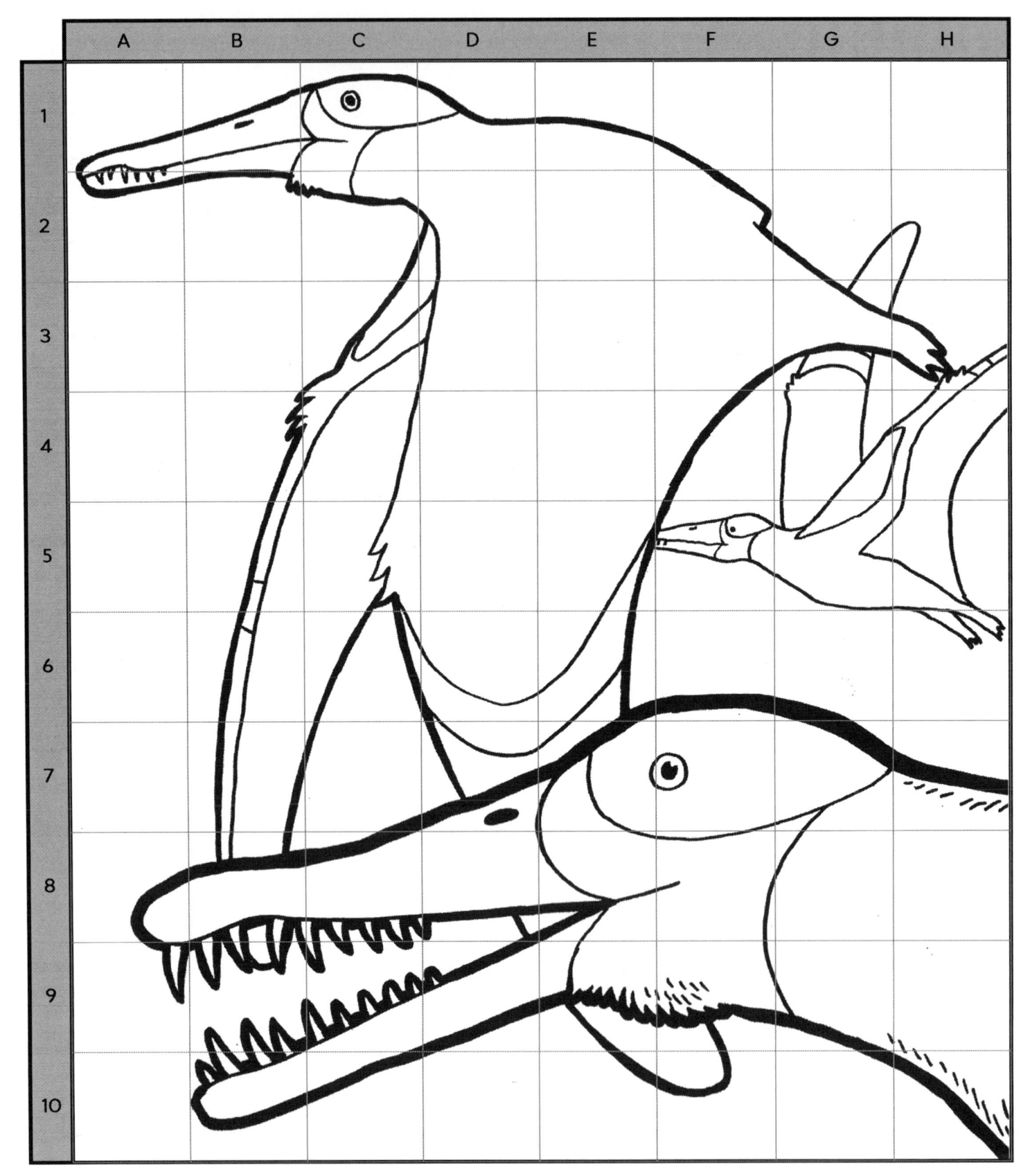

CEARADACTYLUS

112 MYA, Early Cretaceous, Brazil

This pterosaur's long, cone-shaped teeth were suitable for grabbing and holding onto slippery fish. It was a mid-size pterosaur, with a wingspan about 5.5 meters across. Living on the coast, it probably spent its days soaring over waves, and catching fish in mid-flight.

SPINOSAURUS

112-93.5 MYA, Late Jurassic to Early Cretaceous, Egypt

A theropod that is as controversial as it is popular, Spinosaurus was a fish-eating dinosaur that lived in and around shorelines and mudflats. Though its mouth and teeth were shaped to best grasp slippery fish, it would probably not have turned up its nose at other prey, much like the alligators and crocodiles of today.

	A	B	C	D	E	F	G	H
1								
2								
3								
4								
5								
6								
7								
8								
9								
10								

PTERODAUSTRO

105 MYA, Early Cretaceous, Argentina, Chile

A rather small pterosaur, its long jaws were filled with bristle-like teeth that were well-suited for sifting through water for tiny crustaceans. Looking at the scleral rings (a ring-shaped bone that supports the eye), and comparing them to the scleral rings of birds today, it was found to have been nocturnal.

CITIPATI

84-75 MYA, Late Cretaceous, Mongolia

These oviraptorids are commonly used to reconstruct members of the poorly preserved Oviraptors, since more and better quality fossils have been documented. The first Citipati were discovered crouching over their own nests, arms spread across on either side over the eggs. This posture is often found in modern birds, and it was decided that Citipati and other oviraptorids were also covered in feathers.

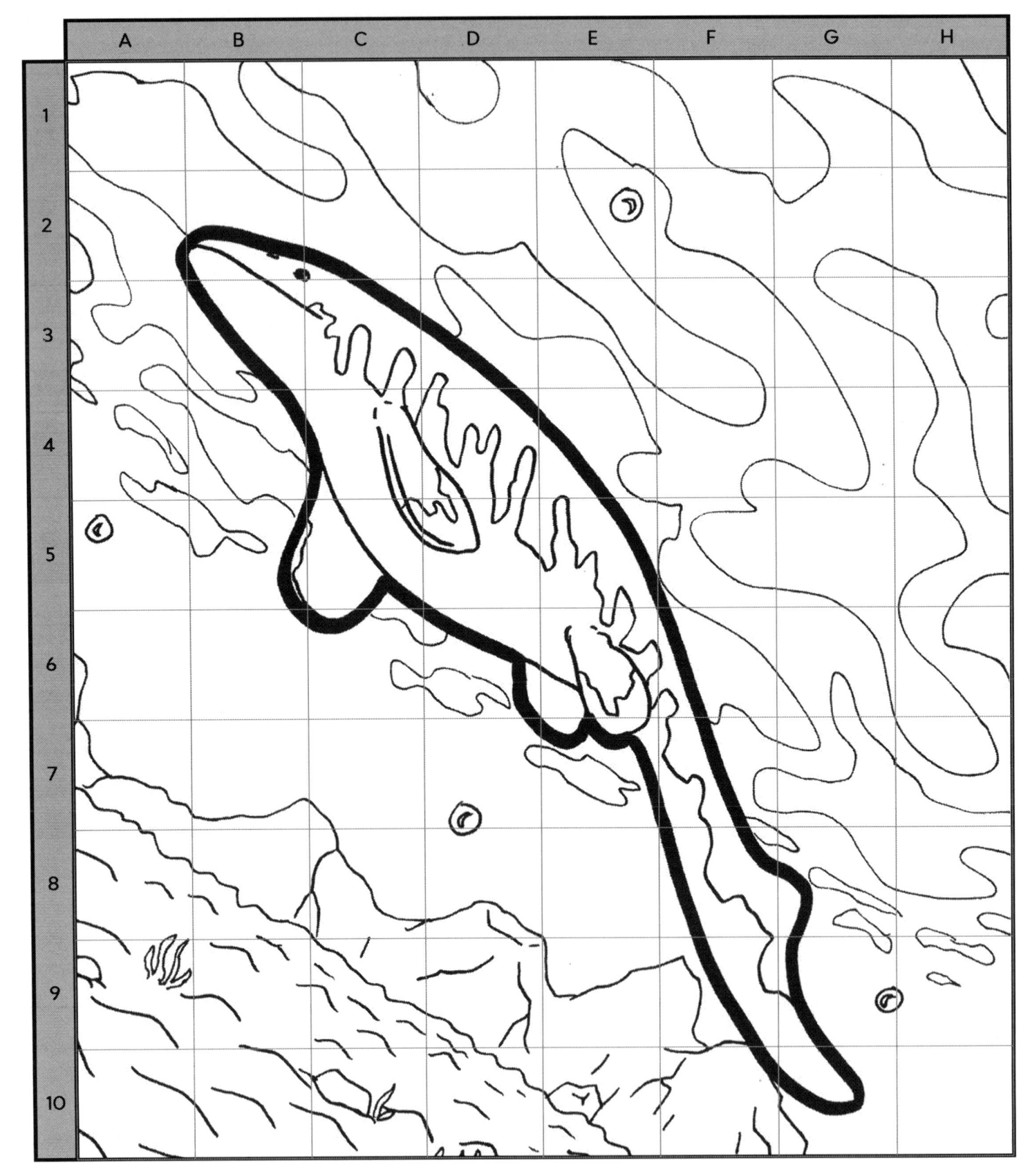

MOSASAURUS

70-66 MYA, Late Cretaceous, North America, Western Europe

This large mosasaur had a preference for big, slow-moving prey. It was very heavily built, and was originally mistaken for another species of mosasaur that did prey upon slow, armored animals. It was among the last of the mosasaurids, living up until the end of the Cretaceous.

	A	B	C	D	E	F	G	H
1								
2								
3								
4								
5								
6								
7								
8								
9								
10								

MAIACETUS

47.5 MYA, Middle Eocene, Pakistan

Since the infant was discovered to have exited head-first, these animals probably gave birth on land, where there would be no risk of the infants drowning. It was roughly dolphin-sized, at 2.5 meters long, and weighing between 280 and 390 kilograms. This animal was an intermediate between the land- and sea-dwelling whale ancestors.

	A	B	C	D	E	F	G	H
1								
2								
3								
4								
5								
6								
7								
8								
9								
10								

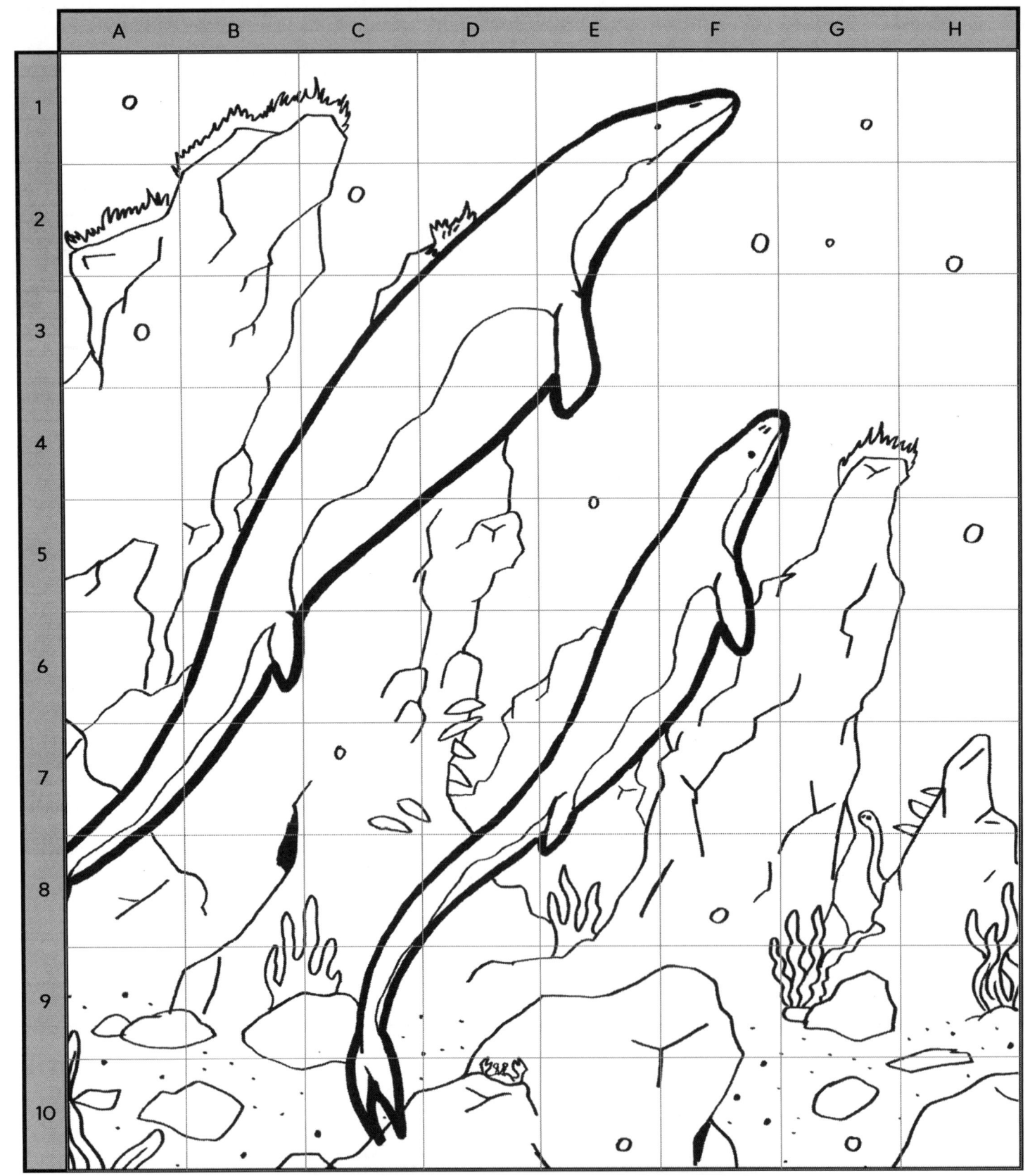

BASILOSAURUS

40-34 MYA, Late Eocene, Egypt, Jordan, United States

Originally thought to have been a large marine reptile, this "lizard king" was an ancestor of the whales we have today. It fed on sharks and other fish, and even other whales. It was not capable of diving as deep as some whales today, or swimming quickly for long periods of time, but it had a powerful bite.

	A	B	C	D	E	F	G	H
1								
2								
3								
4								
5								
6								
7								
8								
9								
10								

Extra practice pages

Extra practice pages

Extra practice pages

Extra practice pages

Extra practice pages

Extra practice pages

Printed in Great Britain
by Amazon